Presenting Christ to Muslims

Presenting Christ to Muslims

Christian Theologians in Dialogue with Muslims

Mark Beaumont

regnum
Mini Book Series

First published 2019 by Regnum Books International

This book is an abridged version of Mark Beaumont's *Christology in Dialogue with Muslims* (Oxford: Regnum, 2005), with thanks to David Cranston for his editorial work.

Regnum is an imprint of the Oxford Centre for Mission Studies
St. Philip and St. James Church
Woodstock Road, Oxford OX2 6HR, UK
www.ocms.ac.uk/regnum

09 08 07 06 05 04 03 7 6 5 4 3 2 1

British Library Cataloguing in Publication Data. A catalogue record for this book is available from the British Library.

ISBN: 978-1-506477-48-0
eBook ISBN: 978-1-506477-49-7

Typeset in Candara by Words by Design.

Photo by Darrell Chaddock on Unsplash

The publication of this volume is made possible through the financial assistance of Evangelisches Missionswerk.

Distributed by 1517 Media in the US and Canada

Contents

Introduction

This book analyses Christian presentations of Christ for Muslims in the most creative periods of Christian-Muslim dialogue, the first half of the ninth and the second half of the twentieth century. In these two historical moments, Christians made a serious effort to present their faith in Christ in terms that take into account Muslim perceptions of him, with a view to bridging the gap between Muslim and Christian convictions. While these Christian writers gave reasons for their own Christological beliefs, they also attempted to argue for their Christology on the basis of Islamic concepts. Rather than merely expound a Christology composed from within a Christian environment, they entered into a Muslim framework of thought to show the validity of a Christian view of Christ in terms that Muslims might understand as credible.

Since Christians and Muslims have such different perceptions of Christ, it may appear to be futile for Christians to try to enter into dialogue with Muslims about him. However, there can be no escape from the fact that Christians understand their identity from the person of Christ, his teaching, and his actions. Indeed the continuing life of the mainstream church has been bound up with the worship of Christ as the eternal Son who became human. Given that Muslims think of Christ as a prophet who brought essentially the same message as Muhammad, that God is one and is to be worshipped alone, they have never understood their identity as being bound up with Christ. In Islam, Christ's words, work and spiritual dynamic were not unique among the messengers of God, but can be seen in other prophets too.

The difficulty of establishing a dialogue is compounded by two denials of Christian faith in Christ: the rejection of the idea of divine sonship, and the denial of the death of Christ by crucifixion. Muslims have not accepted the title 'Son of God' for Christ, and they have held that Christ was taken up to heaven without going through death. These denials cut right to the heart of the developed faith of the church, where Christ is the Incarnate Son of God who gave his life to redeem others from sin. Christians have reacted to these Muslim ideas about Christ in three different ways. Firstly, they have regarded Islam as a completely false ideology and therefore have adopted an aggressive policy of propagating Christian truth without taking Islamic perceptions into account. Secondly, they have distanced themselves from Muslims so that no real communication arises on these contentious issues. Thirdly, they have attempted to take Muslims seriously as people of good faith whose views of Christ need to be understood and related to in a genuine attempt to make sense of Christian faith for them. This third approach is studied here, because it is imperative for Christians to learn to live with Muslims in the global community without falling into the errors of aggression or withdrawal. The approach of peaceful dialogue is a better way than defiant proclamation or complete indifference.

The outstanding Christian presentations of Christ for Muslims came from the ninth and twentieth centuries. By the ninth century, Middle Eastern Christians were engaged in oral and written dialogue with Muslims about their faith in exceedingly detailed terms. The fact of continuing Islamic rule of the largely Christian Middle East led Christian theologians to treat Muslim intellectuals as dialogue partners whom they needed to convince of the rationality of the Christian faith. By this time, the credibility of the Christian faith was at stake, with nominal Christians converting to Islam in increasing numbers. Thus the apologetic writing of the ninth century has both Muslim and Christian audiences in mind. It shows on the one hand that Christology was not completely alien to Islamic belief, and on the other, that it was acceptable for Christians to hold such views even in a society ruled by Muslims.

This book is an abridged version of the larger work that had its origin in a PhD thesis completed at the Oxford Centre for Mission Studies in 2003.

The Islamic Context for Dialogue on Christology

Christian dialogue with Muslims about Christ has always been affected by the portrait of him found in the Qur'ān, which both affirms and denies convictions held about Christ by Christians. The Qur'ān affirms that Christ was born of the virgin Mary, that he had a special measure of God's Spirit, that he healed the sick and raised the dead, and that he brought God's message to his people Israel which confirmed the *Torah* previously given through Moses. In addition, the Qur'ān makes claims about Christ that the Christian gospels do not, that he made a bird from clay, that he predicted Muhammad's coming, and that he was taken up to heaven instead of being put to death. The Qur'ān denies that Christ sought faith in himself, that he should be called God's Son, and that he died by crucifixion.

Thus the Qur'ān affirms, adds to and denies aspects of the life of Christ found in the gospels. The virginal conception is accepted as true but a Christian understanding of the incarnation is ruled out. The miraculous work of Jesus is affirmed, but not a Christian veneration of Jesus' miraculous power as proof of his divinity. His teaching does challenge Jewish convictions, but is essentially the same as that of Moses, since Jesus' authority is no greater than that of previous messengers. In his prophetic teaching he looks forward explicitly to the coming of Muhammad, whose authority he endorses. Christians are wrong to worship Christ since he called on his followers to worship God alone; they are wrong to use language of Jesus that implies a biological link with God, because God cannot be limited to a human level; they are also wrong to claim that Jesus died by crucifixion, because his exaltation bypassed the plans of his enemies.

The implications for Christians of the three denials of the Qur'ān are serious. If Christ did not seek for faith in himself then a major focus of New Testament and subsequent Christian faith is misplaced, and needs to be radically altered in favour of pure monotheism. If God did not have a son then many New Testament texts must be rewritten to avoid making the claim that God is the father of his son Christ. If Christ did not die on the cross then the ending of his life in the four gospels must be adjusted accordingly, and the teaching of the Apostles about the saving effects of his death on the cross must be abandoned.

The following study of Christian dialogue with Muslims about Christ shows how Christian apologists have dealt with these challenges while maintaining a belief in the divinity and humanity of Christ. Since there will be an increasing need for Christians to take the Islamic context into proper account in articulating their faith in a plural world, consideration of the most creative responses to these challenges should enable them to "give a reason for (their) hope in a gracious and respectful way".

The Beginning of Dialogue on Christology in the Eighth Century

The arrival of Muslim rule in the traditionally Christian sectors of the Middle East, in the fourth decade of the seventh century, brought a direct challenge to the churches to give an account of Christ in the light of the Islamic understanding of him. If the Qur'ān offered a correct account of Christ, then Christians would sooner or later have to defend their conviction that Jesus Christ was the eternal Son of God who had become human to rescue humanity from the results of sin through his death on the cross. Incarnation and atonement were at the heart of Christian faith but these central doctrines were under attack from the new religion that had taken control over this section of the Christian world. The denials of the incarnation and the atonement by the new rulers forced Christians to account for these doctrines, not only to those who regarded them as false, but also to nominal Christians who were adopting the new religion. This task was made more complicated by the fact that Middle Eastern Christians were divided into three communities characterised by particular Christologies. These were the Chalcedonian churches including the Melkites, the Jacobites and the Nestorians. Melkites were the Christians of Syria and Egypt who accepted the ruling of the Council of Chalcedon (451) affirming the two natures – divine and human – of Christ in one hypostasis or substance. The Jacobites were named after Jacob Baradaeus who became a rallying point for those who opposed the two natures definition of Chalcedon, holding to the unity of both the substance and nature. The Nestorians refused to confess that Mary was the mother of God, and claimed that the Messiah had two natures and two hypostases. Muslim intellectuals could easily charge Christians with incoherent interpretations of Christ by these three groups that stood in need of a simpler and more rational treatment.

By the late eight and early ninth centuries Christian theologians from each of the three communities were producing Christological writing of great sophistication. This was mainly due to a climate of intellectual exchange between thinking Muslims and Christians that would not be paralleled until modern times. During this period Muslim intellectuals were studying the Greek heritage passed on to them by Christians who were engaged in translating Greek texts into Arabic. The openess of Muslims to the cultural values of Christians provided a basis for two-way communication between the rulers and those ruled. By the end of the ninth century Muslim attitudes to Christians had narrowed to such an extent that creative dialogue had become circumscribed and Christians found themselves marginalised from public intellectual discourse.

While there are indications of dialogue about Christ between Muslims and Christians from the seventh century, the earliest known written defence of Christian belief about Christ comes from John of Damascus (d. c. 750), after his retirement from service in the Muslim government in the second decade of the eighth century. John was a member of the Greek speaking churches that followed the Christological affirmations of the councils of Ephesus (431, affirming the Nicene Creed and condemning the teaching of the Nestorians), and Chalcedon (451, affirming that Jesus was perfect in deity and humanness, both God and man). John was later to be regarded as one of the doctors of the Eastern Orthodox churches for his systematic account of the faith. He referred to Islam as one of many heresies of his era, which may reflect a widespread view of the new movement among Christians.

An anonymous defence of the Christian doctrines of the trinity and the incarnation in Arabic came from the Greek speaking Chalcedonian churches in Palestine, possibly before 750, showing that Christians were beginning to adopt the language of Islam at least to engage in debate with Muslims. It was most probably the work of the monastic communities of South Palestine, which John had joined after his retirement, that shows a familiarity with the Qur'ān thus demonstrating a willingness to approach Muslims on their terms in order to uphold Christian truth.

From the eighth decade of the century comes the written report of a dialogue between the Caliph al Mahdī and Timothy, the Patriarch of the Nestorian churches in Baghdad. Timothy was invited by al-Mahdī to give an account of a range of Christian beliefs that differed from Islamic teaching. Timothy's grasp of Muslim thought is evidence of a climate of dialogue cultivated by the early `Abbasid Caliphs in which Muslim and Christian theologians developed extensive knowledge of each other's beliefs. The dialogue has been preserved in Syriac and in Arabic, and for the most part shows Timothy offering answers to al-Mahdī's questions, with occasional counter-questions raised by Timothy.

John of Damascus: Dialogue with Muslims about Christ

During his retirement from public office, John wrote three treatises, which he put together under the title *Pege Gnosis* 'The Fount of Knowledge'. The first treatise, *Dialectica*, is a study of philosophy, the second, *De Haeresibus*, describes one hundred heresies, and includes answers to questions posed by Muslims on the trinity, the incarnation and scripture while the third, *De Fide Orthodoxa*, expounds orthodox belief.

John firstly recognised the way Muslims see Christ. Rather than repeat the affirmations of Orthodox Christology, he builds his case on foundations acceptable to Muslims. While they refuse to speak of him as God's son, they call Christ God's word and spirit. John begins his answer to the question about sonship with this Muslim affirmation about Christ. If Christ is word and spirit from God, then surely he shares attributes of God in such a way that makes him divine as well as human.

Secondly, John avoids areas of outright denial – thus he does not discuss why Christians call Jesus God's Son. He also declines to appeal to Christian scripture, since he is aware of Muslim hesitation about the authenticity of the text and rather than appeal to the authority of the sacred text, John counsels Christians to develop arguments that depend on ideas acceptable to Muslims themselves with a view to reaching Christian conclusions. This type of apologetic argument that seeks to make a reasonable case for Christology on grounds acceptable to Muslims flourishes more fully in the early ninth century, as discussed in later chapters.

Dialogue between the Caliph Al-Mahdī and the Nestorian Patriarch Timothy I

This dialogue, which took place shortly after Timothy became Patriarch of the Nestorian church in Mesopotamia in 780, exists in Syriac and Arabic. The Caliph asks most of the questions, allowing Timothy the occasional counter-question, scrutinising Timothy's understanding of the trinity, the incarnation, and the Bible.

This dialogue graphically displays the concerns Muslims have with Christian faith in Christ. Firstly, Muslims suspect that there is a biological link between Jesus and God in the thinking of Christians, which undermines the character of God. Secondly, the idea that Christ has two natures seems to the Muslim mind to be a logical impossibility, since it would result in two separate beings rather than one. Thirdly, the Christian claim that Christ died on the cross proves the logical absurdity of the two natures concept, because it ought rationally to follow that both natures died there and not just the human. Finally, the supposed death of Christ by crucifixion must undermine both the dignity of Christ's status as a prophet and the power of God to protect him.

Timothy's method is to avoid giving offence at all costs in the way that he answers the Caliph's questions. Thus he never criticises the Qur'ān as such but only the Caliph's interpretation of particular Qur'ānic texts.

Towards Ninth Century Dialogue on Christology

From John's cryptic advice to Christians in their conversation with Muslims to the detailed debate between Timothy and al-Mahdī is a journey short in time but long in theological development. John wrote in Greek for Christians. *The Anonymous Apology* in the middle of the eighth century was an Arabic document for Christians with a Muslim readership in mind. Timothy's dialogue would have been conducted in Arabic, and the Arabic text would have been produced for Muslims as well as for Christians.

The Anonymous Apology presents a Christology based on the Bible with some Christological language taken from the Nicene creed and the Chalcedonian definition. However, the treatise does not give a Muslim response to the Christology put forward. Timothy, on the contrary, was required to answer questions about Christological ideas that were unacceptable to Muslims, so he was forced by the circumstances of the interview to mount a defence of Christology as best he could. Timothy's apologetic method of giving reasoned answers to difficult questions was further developed by the three ninth century apologists, Abū Qurra, Abū Rā'iṯa and `Ammār al-Baṣrī, whose work will be examined in the following chapters.

The Christology of Theodore Abū Qurra in Dialogue with Muslims

Theodore Abū Qurra

Abū Qurra (c.755-c.829) was the leading Middle Eastern Chalcedonian theologian in the generation after John of Damascus, but little is known about his life, apart from a few details given in two Syriac Chronicles, *The Chronicle of Michael The Syrian*, and *The Anonymous Chronicle of 1234*. The former mentions that Theodore was Bishop of Harrān in Syria before being deposed by the Patriarch Theodoret of Antioch, and that he travelled to Egypt and Armenia around 813-4 to promote Chalcedonian orthodoxy. Patriarch Theodoret was in office between 785 and 799 and therefore Theodore probably was Bishop of Harrān sometime during those years. The latter chronicle says that Abū Qurra was involved in a debate with the Caliph al-Ma'mūn (813-833) in the year 829. Sidney Griffith adds together these biographical items to give a career spanning 40 years, assuming he was 30 years of age in 785.

Among his writings are a number of apologetic treatises for Jews, Muslims and Christians concerning Christology. For Christians, he defended the Chalcedonian definition against those who did not accept it. For Jews, he attempted to show that Jesus was superior to Moses in his ability to perform miracles in his own name so proving that he was divine. For Muslims, he produced at least three treatises on Christology. These are concerned with the problem of attributing incarnation to God, the nature of the Sonship of Christ, and the necessity of the suffering of Christ for the forgiveness of sin. The existence of treatises in Arabic addressed to such a variety of audiences shows how the language of Islam had, by the turn of the ninth century, become the common means of discourse in the Middle East. His treatise comparing Moses and Jesus assumes that Jewish readers understand Arabic. His *Confession of the Orthodox Faith* is essentially a catechetical piece to educate fellow Melkite Christians in the errors of alternative Christologies and the rightness of the definition of Chalcedon. This is written in complex theological language designed for serious students of theology, perhaps indicating that the traditional Church languages of Greek and Syriac were giving way to Arabic.

Answering questions Muslims ask Christians was firstly an aid to fellow Christians in their encounter with Muslims, and secondly a means of making Christian faith more understandable to Muslims. Abū Qurra seems to have been successful in reaching a Muslim audience, given that among others `Īsā ibn Sabīh al-Murdār (d. 840) wrote a refutation of his writing entitled *Kitāb `alā Abī Qurra al-nasrānī* (Against Abū Qurra the Christian), which is unfortunately no longer extant.

In order to discover to what extent Abū Qurra developed his Christology as a result of dialogue with Muslims, his *Confession of the Orthodox Faith* written for a Christian audience may be compared with the three apologetic pieces for Muslims. The comparison shows that while not developing new Christological concepts in dialogue, Abū Qurra did provide arguments for Christological beliefs that were based on principles derived from Islamic teaching.

Confession of the Orthodox Faith

This confession is written as a statement of faith with the formula "I believe" along with refutations of several unorthodox views, suiting a catechetical purpose. Even though it is an Arabic tract, it does not address Muslims, nor does it allude to Islamic concerns with Christology. In the three treatises for Muslims on Christ, however, the content shifts from confession of faith to apologetic, from argument with other Christians to argument with Muslims, from defence of the Chalcedonian definition to defence of the possibility that the divine became human. The Islamic understanding of Christ was now forcing theologians to mount a much more elaborate defence of Christology than had been attempted before. The first of these treatises is a response to the Muslim view that if God is transcendent then the embodiment of the divine is impossible, and if Christ suffered then he cannot be divine.

A Reply to the One who Refuses to Attribute the Incarnation to God

This apology attempts to answer a question raised by Muslims about the incarnation and is one of the first known attempts to argue for the possibility of the incarnation with Muslims who denied it.

By appealing to two notions familiar to Muslims, God's session on a throne, and the perfection of Christ's character, he argues that Muslims can believe in the incarnation on terms acceptable to them. This is an apologetics of persuasion, which appeals to concepts held by the dialogue partner. What Abū Qurra succeeds in doing here is to present incarnation in a way that takes seriously Muslim reservations, so that the idea of incarnation may not simply be dismissed as fantastic nonsense.

God Has a Son Who Is His Equal in Nature and Who Exists Forever with Him

In this apology Abū Qurra deals with the alleged problem of God giving birth to a son. However, the Muslim denial of fatherhood for God prevents any proper discussion of the sonship of Christ, and Abū Qurra realises that the prior question of the nature of God himself needs to be answered before any purely Christological discussion can proceed with Muslims. In the Bible, God's wisdom seems to have personal, almost human characteristics, yet is an aspect of God's nature. On this basis God's son has individual human characteristics but still is fully identified with God's nature. If Muslims can accept the personification of God's wisdom, then it should not be too difficult for them to appreciate the union of divine nature with human nature in Christ. While the appeal to the hearing and seeing of God is based on Qur'ānic concepts, here the appeal to wisdom is not.

There is No Forgiveness for Sin without the Suffering of the Messiah on Behalf of Humanity

In this treatise Abū Qurra questions the Islamic belief that God's forgiveness can be obtained directly without the help of an intermediary. His aim is to show the necessity of the sacrificial death of Christ by spelling out the conditions laid down in the Bible, based on the premise that God must judge sin rather than overlook it. Christ provides the way for God to forgive without forsaking justice. Whether Muslims would be impressed with such an argument is doubtful given the denials of the crucifixion of Christ and human ransom for sin in the Qur'ān, and his argument for the death of Christ as an atonement for sin would most probably fail to convince a Muslim.

Conclusion

Abū Qurra's Christology in dialogue with Muslims is largely a defence of the Nicene-Chalcedonian tradition. He translates the orthodox creeds into Arabic, finding terminology to suit the truth of that Christology for Muslims.

His two treatises on incarnation and sonship are constructed on a dialogical framework of "you ask, and we reply". The burden of his apologetic Christology for Muslims was not so much exposition and defence of received tradition, but more a defence of Christology mounted on Islamic principles. Thus in the three apologies for Muslims, there is no discussion of varieties of Christological positions held by Christians. He was trying to find openings in Muslim thought for the presentation of Christ as he saw him. His contemporary Abū

Rā'iṯa, with whom he debated concerning Christology, took this method to a more sophisticated level in his apologetic writing for Muslims.

The Christology of H̲abīb ibn Khidma Abū Rā'iṯa in Dialogue with Muslims

H̲abīb ibn Khidma Abū Rā'iṯa was a Jacobite theologian associated with Takrit to the north west of Baghdad. He was a contemporary of Abū Qurra, with whom he claims to have debated face to face. He was named in The Chronicle of Michael the Syrian as a participant in a synod held in the year 828, so probably was active beyond the third decade of the ninth century.

Syriac was probably Abū Rā'iṯa's native language, although like Abū Qurra, he wrote in Arabic which was a necessity, not just for communication with Muslims, but also between Melkites and Jacobites. His *Demonstration of the Christian Religion and the Holy Trinity* dealt with only one Muslim concern, while the *Letter on the Incarnation* opens up eleven areas of Muslim unease about Christology. When these questions are compared with those posed by the Melkites in the treatises addressed to them by Abū Rā'iṯa, it becomes apparent how the Islamic context radically changed the way Christology had to be discussed.

Appeals to Islamic convictions are more penetrating in the writing of Abū Rā'iṯa than that of Abū Qurra. The use of Islamic beliefs enabled him to show that Christian belief about the incarnation is not entirely incompatible with Islamic belief, even if he was probably unable to show any necessary connection between the incarnation and Islamic thought. He develops a very thorough apologetic for the possibility of incarnation that had not been part of the traditional intra-Christian Christological debates that had run for centuries. While Abū Qurra fields a few questions raised by Muslims about the divine becoming human, Abū Rā'iṯa attempts an encyclopaedic survey of all the issues Muslims raise on the topic. His answers show a patient seriousness with questions that Christians take for granted, and provide a model for Christians in any age in their dialogue with Muslims.

Abū Rā'iṯa was not alone in developing an extensive apologetic on Christology in the early ninth century. The following chapter will examine a similar type of writing by `Ammār al-Baṣrī, a Nestorian theologian who was probably a younger contemporary of Abū Rā'iṯa and Abū Qurra.

The Christology of `Ammār al-Baṣrī in Dialogue with Muslims

`Ammār al-Basrī

`Ammār al-Baṣrī came from the Nestorian church, and was an apologist in the early ninth century and a contemporary of the Muslim scholar Abū l-Hudhayl al-`Allāf (d. c. 840) who wrote a "refutation of `Ammār the Christian". The fact that he wrote in Arabic signals a development in Nestorian apologetic writing from the late eighth century when Timothy's debate with the Caliph al-Mahdī held in 781-2 was first written in Syriac and then translated into Arabic. The Nestorian community was using the language of the ruling power by the beginning of the ninth century.

The two surviving works by `Ammār are apologetic treatises. His *Book of the Proof* covers the key areas of controversy between Christians and Muslims with most attention paid to explaining the trinity and the incarnation. `Ammār's *Book of Questions and Answers* deals with the Christian understanding of revelation, the four gospels, the trinity and the incarnation. This latter work is dedicated to the Caliph, most likely al-Ma'mūn, who ruled from 813 to 833.

The Book of the Proof

`Ammār writes in a dialogical style offering a defence of Christianity in the light of Muslim interrogation. However, the addressees are Christians rather than Muslims since Christians are 'we' and Muslims 'they' throughout the book, and the pamphlet would seem to be a compendium of ready reference for Christians who are involved in religious controversy with Muslims on a day-to-day basis.

`Ammār shares with Abū Qurra and Abū Rā'iṯa similar vocabulary to describe the incarnation, and like Abū Rā'iṯa he understands the eternal Word to have fashioned a human nature for himself from the human issue from Mary. Unlike Abū Qurra and Abū Rā'iṯa, `Ammār argues that the purity of Christ is not guaranteed by the creation of a sinless human nature before the union of the divine and human natures. Rather, the sinless Incarnate one had to prove his obedience to the divine will right to the end of his earthly life, since only at the end could he be pronounced pure of any kind of wrongdoing.

The theme of testing is significant in the Christology of `Ammār, for he painstakingly argues for the unfolding obedience of Christ as if disobedience was a real possibility. Indeed, it is this struggle to obey the will of God that gives `Ammār's Christ a real human nature, despite the metaphors that imply the opposite. The apologetic value of the testing of Christ would have been considerable, since the fact that Christ is tested by God would have enabled Muslims to recognize a human Christ in `Ammār's presentation more readily than in any of the others from the eighth and ninth centuries. Even his fellow Nestorian, Timothy I, did not argue for the continued testing of Christ in his debate with al-Mahdī. Since `Ammār allowed for a dynamic interchange between divinity and humanity in the life experiences of Christ, his presentation was an advance on the apologetic alternatives on offer in the early ninth century.

`Ammār used three analogies for the purpose of the incarnation in the *Book of Questions and Answers* which were excellent means of communication with Muslims. The parable of the king having his son born among his people who then brings the people into his father's inheritance shows the loving identification of God with humans that the incarnation seeks to uphold. The prizefighter who exhausts himself in defeating his opponent, and the doctor who takes poison before giving it to his patient, show the lengths to which God is prepared to go to rescue humans from death, the key idea behind the death of Christ. These stories expound the importance of the incarnation and the atonement in imaginative ways that would probably have made a favorable impression on Muslims.

`Ammār's presentation of the death of Christ is original and compelling in three respects. Firstly, in *The Book of the Proof* he argues that the humiliation of Christ, so unacceptable to Muslims, can be mitigated by the honour he is given by God as a result of his defeat of death. Therefore the shame of his crucifixion is outweighed by the glory he is able to grant to other humans whose death is transcended as a result of the cross. Muslims may have been able to perceive that someone who lays down his life in a shameful fashion could give honour to others in the process, and so be praised for seeking the greater glory of others. Secondly, his distinction between divine attributes related to Christ's human nature and others that are separate helps to hold together the divine and human natures of Christ at his death. If eternity is not imparted to the humanity of

Christ then it is not lost at death, as Muslims may think must be the case. On the other hand, if God's power and authority are imparted to his humanity then these are lost at the point of death. There is a temporary loss of these divine attributes between the time of death and the resurrection of Christ in God's power and authority. This is a distinction unique to `Ammār, which goes a long way to answering the question also asked in the writing of Timothy, Abū Qurra and Abū Rā'iṯa – how it is that the divine nature can die, without losing control of the created world? Whereas the other three apologists simply deny that the divine dies and that only the human experiences death, `Ammār shows that some aspects of divinity can cease to be part of Christ at death. However, the fundamental characteristic of God's nature, his eternity, is unaffected by death. This dialectical Christology is much more flexible in an Islamic context than the more rigid separation of divine and human found in the apologetics of Timothy, Abū Qurra and Abū Rā'iṯa.

Thirdly, his emphasis on the resurrection of Christ as a guarantee that death can be overcome for others is unique amongst eighth and ninth century apologists. The weakness of any theoretical offer of life beyond death lies in the lack of assurance that it will actually happen, but this is not the case for those who believe that Christ went through death into a new life. Here is the evidence that others can follow him after death into life. Such an indirect challenge to Muslims to see if they have similar evidence for their resurrection is met with the idea that Christ was raised without going through death, but `Ammār points out that humans need to be assured that death will not overcome them. It is altogether more reassuring for the rest of humanity if Christ did die before being raised to life. Here `Ammār has shown that in the resurrection of Christ there is a promise that humans can rely on.

These distinctive arguments show both that `Ammār was searching for creative ways to defend the two natures Christology inherited from his Nestorian tradition and that he was prepared to develop new ways of forming Christology in the context of dialogue with Muslims. The new developments are seen in the emphasis placed on the testing of the human nature of Christ, and in the distinctions between types of divine attributes that impacted Christ's human nature. Even if Muslims appreciated the rounded human portrait of Christ offered here, they probably were not convinced by the equation of divine attributes of power and authority at work in Christ with the actual presence of God in him. Nevertheless, `Ammār's presentation of Christ for Muslims is the most comprehensive in his epoch, offering a more detailed treatment than Abū Rā'iṯa of the issues facing Christians in their understanding of Christ in a Muslim context.

The Christologies of Abū Qurra, Abū Rā'iṯa and `Ammār al-Baṣrī and Muslim Response

Christian apologists in the early `Abbasid period were concerned to uphold the non-contradictory nature of the incarnation. Both Abū Rā'iṯa and Abū Qurra present the eternal Word as uniting with human flesh from Mary, with the result that there was one nature consisting of divine and human characteristics. In his *Letter on the Incarnation* Abū Rā'iṯa presents arguments which attempt to show the reasonableness of the incarnation to Muslims in the light of Islamic convictions. Unlike Abū Qurra, he is explicit about the nature of Muslim thought, with the presupposition that, properly understood, a Christian view of Christ is not incompatible with Islamic conceptions of him.

On the other hand `Ammār al-Baṣrī's known Christological writing is addressed to Muslims. He believes that a Nestorian Christology is less susceptible to Muslim objections than rival ones. It is almost as if the Nestorian is grateful to Islam for providing a platform for re-instating the anathematised Nestorian teaching to its rightful place as the truth.

Muslim Responses to Christian Views of Christ in the Ninth and Tenth Centuries

The Truth about Christ Comes from the Qur'ān

The first type of response was to appeal to the Qur'ān as the measure by which to judge Christian beliefs. This was the approach of al-Qāsim ibn Ibrāhīm al-Hasanī al-Rassī (d. 860) who wrote a *Reply to the Christians* possibly in the period from 815 to 826, during which he debated with Christians in Egypt – probably the earliest surviving Muslim writing against Christian beliefs. Al-Qāsim documents the three main Christian presentations of the incarnation by Melkites, Jacobites and Nestorians before concluding that all of them depart from the teaching of "the prophets and apostles of God".

Christian Scriptures do not Support the Incarnation

A second type of critique made by `Alī ibn Rabbān al-Tabarī (d. 855) and al-Nāshi al-Akbar (d. 904) was to separate developed Christology from that found in the Bible in order to show that Christian thought had forsaken its roots. `Alī al-Tabarī claimed to have been a Christian for 70 years, before converting to Islam, and in his *Reply to the Christians*, which must have been written sometime around the middle of the ninth century his familiarity with the Bible is evident.

He writes that the Bible presents a human rather than a divine Christ, and the father-son terminology found in the gospels has been radically changed by developed Christological formulations into something it was not intended to mean. As such he blames Christians for superimposing Greek philosophical categories on the language of the gospels.

Arguments for the Incarnation are Incoherent

A third type of response was to deny the validity of the apologetics put forward by Christians to defend the incarnation. Abū `Īsā al-Warrāq (d. 861) and Abū Bakr Mu̱hammad ibn al-Ṯayyib al-Bāqillānī (d. 1014) argued that Christian explanations for the incarnation were inadequate because the notion of the union of the divine with the human was incoherent, further observing that Nestorians, Jacobites and Melkites are not consistent in the way they describe the humanity of Christ.

Conclusion

The developments in Christology are seen in the arguments to commend the rationality of the incarnation as understood by Abū Qurra the Melkite, Abū Rā'iṯa the Jacobite, and `Ammār the Nestorian. The first two shared a common concern to argue for the incarnation on Islamic grounds, while `Ammar was more inclined to present arguments that showed the value of the incarnation as a means of the revelation of God, although he did also develop some distinctive arguments based on Islamic ideas. Abū Qurra and `Ammār were less inclined to adopt Islamic terminology, preferring to explain the meaning of their Christological traditions in ways that might be intelligible to Muslims.

The response by Muslim authors illustrates the way such arguments were received, but the fact that al-Bāqillānī took the trouble to refute such arguments in the second half of the tenth century shows that Muslim intellectuals felt the force of the Christian case made over a century before. This may suggest that arguments based on Islamic premises can have a continuing usefulness to Christian apologists.

What does remain relevant to the twenty-first century is the attempt to show the coherence of the incarnation on Islamic terms and for modern Christians who continue to uphold the incarnation, the models provided by these three ninth century apologists still have value.

New Beginnings in the Nineteenth and Early Twentieth Centuries

Between the Ninth and Nineteenth Centuries

In between the ninth and twentieth centuries lies a period of increasing distance between Muslims and Christians. By the end of the ninth century Muslim intellectuals had abandoned debate with Christians on the grounds that everything that can be known about revealed truth was contained in Islam, and that Christian conceptions of revelation were not only inadequate but subversive to the truth of the oneness of God. Christians in the Islamic world continued to decline in numbers as many born into Christian families converted to Islam. Such a demographic shift meant that the self-confidence of the Christian communities also declined, as the distance between Muslim and Christian intellectuals grew wider. The arrival of the Mongols in the Middle East after 1259 led to the systematic oppression of Middle Eastern Christians, which became particularly intense under Tīmūr Lang from 1394 to 1405 when Christians in the Mesopotamian region who did not convert to Islam were hunted down.

Christians beyond the Muslim Empire looked on Muslims as a military threat for many centuries. European Christians typically saw Islam as the Antichrist seeking to engulf Christian Europe just as once the Christian Middle East had been overrun. The few European Christians who attempted to understand Islam did so from an antagonistic base. Not until the academic study of Islam in the eighteenth century did Europeans approach Islam from a more reasoned and sympathetic point of view. Missionaries to the Muslim world from Europe began to debate with Muslims in terms of the academic study of Islam, and this culminated in twentieth century Christian theologians attempting to study theology from a global rather than a western perspective. The encounter of Christians from beyond the Muslim world with Islam has been difficult, but as the twenty-first century opens, there is a more lively concern to be Christians in an Islamic context than ever before. Muslims have continued to hold Christians responsible for undermining the unity of God, and relatively few have sought to debate with Christians on the incarnation and atonement.

Between the creative period of the late eighth and early ninth centuries little dialogue took place with the notable exception of the contribution made in the twelfth century by Paul of Antioch, Melkite Bishop of Sidon, who quoted extensively from the Qur'ān in support of the Gospel accounts of Christ in his *Letter to the Muslims*.

During the Medieval period, the European Christian encounter with Islam was coloured by the threat posed by possible Muslim invasion. Those who attempted to understand Islam did not engage in the kind of apologetic used by Middle Eastern Christians, but sought to directly criticise Islam in the light of Christian truth. Nicholas of Cusa (1401-1464) made the greatest effort in the West to read the Qur'ān sympathetically, while the arrival of Jesuits in

Northwest India in the sixteenth century provided a new opportunity for engagement with Islam. They were able to hold discussions with the Mughal Emperor Akbar on a variety of topics, including the incarnation and crucifixion of Christ. However, it was not until the nineteenth century that European Christian mission was able to produce apologetic work that addressed Muslims in terms of their own scholarly tradition. By then, developments in the study of Islam by European scholars had become available for apologetic use. The fruit of this knowledge can be seen in the writing of Karl Pfander (1803-1868), whose training in Islamic studies in Switzerland enabled him to engage in debate with Muslims by quoting Muslim scholars to support Christian interpretation of the Qur'ān.

Karl Pfander's The Balance of Truth

Karl Pfander was a Pietistic Lutheran from Germany who joined the Basel Mission to work among Muslims on the northern border of Persia. His presentation of Christianity entitled *The Balance of Truth* was published in Armenian in 1831, Persian in 1835, and Urdu in 1843 (after he moved to India in 1841). Pfander wrote the work to fill a gap in literature for the Muslim audience he encountered in preaching around Shusha in the Caucasus and on trips within Persia. Few of his missionary contemporaries had read the Qur'ān or Islamic writing. Henry Martyn was one who had, but he had dedicated his energy to scripture translation before his death in 1812 at the age of 31. Pfander was attempting to communicate the Christian faith in terms a Muslim might understand, rather than simply repeat the theological terminology he had learned in Europe.

The Balance of Truth first addresses the authenticity of the Old and New Testaments, since Pfander had discovered that this was the most important point of contention in discussions with Muslims. If he could persuade his reader of the trustworthiness of Christian scripture then the trinity and the incarnation which he goes on to expound, would be firmly grounded. Pfander declined to debate these doctrines in isolation from their origin in revelation. His presentation of Christian claims about Jesus follows a detailed argument showing that the *Torah* and the *Injīl* had not been corrupted by Jews or Christians. Pfander's Protestant background shows through in his opening emphasis on the Apostolic conviction that Christ died to save sinners. To support this he ranges widely over the New Testament teaching on the atonement. His appeal to the Qur'ān commentator al-Baidāwī (d.c. 1290) and others marks a new stage in Christian apologetic writing for Muslims. He presents evidence from Islamic sources to back up Christian claims about Jesus.

Rahmatullāh al-Kairānawī, who saw himself as a defender of Islam, challenged Pfander to deal with the status of the Bible, the trinity, the Prophethood of Muhammad, and the status of the Qur'ān in a public debate in Agra in 1854. This introduced a new dimension to dialogue between Christians and Muslims. Pfander had not read Strauss' *The Life of Jesus* before the debate and had been largely unaware of critical European gospel scholarship that had been engaged in the task of separating the Christ of history from the Christ of the faith of the Church. It would now be difficult for Christian missionaries to avoid the work of Christian scholars in the way that Pfander had, because Muslims could produce literature liberally quoting the findings of such scholarship. The future path of dialogue on Christology was now established, but Pfander did not himself embark on it.

Ibrāhīm Lūqā's Christianity in Islam

Pfander's method of using Islamic sources to defend Christian belief was taken much further by an Egyptian Coptic priest, Ibrāhīm Lūqā, in the following century. His *Christianity in Islam*, first published in 1938, was into its third printing in 1967 when it was banned by the Egyptian authorities. Lūqā's treatment of Christ takes in the whole of the Qur'ānic portrait, paying particular attention to the way well known commentators understood the Christ of the Qur'ān, with the aim of demonstrating that Christian teaching is not incompatible with that of the Qur'ān. His adoption of Pfander's apologetic method shows that not only Western missionaries were inclined to try to read the Qur'ān in a Christian way. Unlike Pfander, Lūqā avoids any direct criticism of the Prophet, but his work is basically the same format as Pfander's *The Balance of Truth*, since Lūqā also recognises the importance of establishing the authenticity of the sources of Christian faith in the face of Muslim allegation of the corruption of the Bible. His extensive use of well-known commentators on the Qur'ān marks a fresh development in dialogue that goes beyond Pfander's limited use of them, and shows the importance for Christians of paying close attention to Islamic thought. In many respects Lūqā's work represents the fruit of a new attitude among Christians to the careful study of Islam which would become the basis for dialogue in the second half of the twentieth century.

Muslim Reactions to Christology in the Nineteenth and Early Twentieth Centuries

Two Indian and two Egyptian writers have been chosen as representative of a variety of responses to Christian views of Jesus. The two Indian writers from the nineteenth century were both replying to Pfander, one very negatively and the other much more positively. The first Egyptian writer finds the New Testament portrait of Jesus contradictory, while the second finds much to admire in that portrait. The first Indian Muslim response came from Rahmatullāh al-Kairanāwī (1818-1891) who debated publicly with Pfander and published pamphlets and a book refuting his arguments. The second Indian, Sayyid Aḫmad Khān (1817-1898), took a positive view of the Christian gospels, but argued that they support neither a divine Jesus nor a Christ crucified for the sin of humanity.

Muḫammad `Abdūh (1849-1905), the first of the two Egyptian writers, was one of the leading Muslim thinkers of the late nineteenth century. His criticisms of the Jesus of the Christian gospels have had a significant impact on subsequent Muslim thought. The second Egyptian, Muḫammad Kāmil Husain (1901-77), was a medical practitioner in Cairo who published widely on religious subjects, and became well-known for his 1954 novel on the events of Good Friday in Jerusalem, entitled *City of Wrong*, which led to an Egyptian State Prize for Literature in 1957. He is much more sympathetic to the portrait of Jesus in the gospels, although in his book he stops short of portraying the crucifixion itself. His openness to Coptic Christians results in an appreciation of their faith in Jesus, but a Muslim cannot look to Jesus as more than an exemplar. Husain was asked by his English translator, Kenneth Cragg, what his attitude was to the crucifixion of Jesus recounted in the gospels, and he replied that the Qur'ānic text concerning the crucifixion is difficult to interpret with assurance. In a later book, *The Hallowed Valley*, he expounds why Islam denies the death of Jesus on the cross. Indeed the conflict between Muslims and Christians concerning the death of Christ runs much deeper than many imagine.

Conclusion

Pfander and Lūqā show how Christians could take Islamic convictions into their Christological writing in a partial way. The Muslim writers surveyed show a mixed attitude to Christian scripture and tradition from the generous attitude of Aḫmad Khān to the hostile approach of Rahmatullāh. However, the findings of gospel scholarship enabled both of them to separate the developed faith of the church from the teaching and practice of Jesus of Nazareth, and argue for a Christ that appeared to be much closer to the Qur'ānic portrait than most Christians cared to acknowledge. Neither Pfander nor Lūqā were ready for this reaction, since post-enlightenment gospel scholarship did not contribute to their understanding of Christology. They were essentially locked into a pre-enlightenment framework of scripture interpretation and were incapable of interacting with newer approaches to Christ.

During the second half of the twentieth century this deficit was made up by Christians who realised that dialogue with Muslims about Christ simply had to be conducted on the basis of sound interpretation of the gospels. The following chapter analyses the contribution of Kenneth Cragg, whose portrait of Christ is based on his understanding of the historical Jesus rather than the Christ of the Church's faith.

The Christology of Kenneth Cragg in Dialogue with Muslims

Getting Back to the Historical Jesus

The Christological writing of Kenneth Cragg (1913-2012) spans much of the second half of the twentieth century. His approach to Christology is quite different from any of the apologists reviewed so far, since he bases his understanding of Christ on the records found in the synoptic gospels, rather than on the theology of the fourth gospel, or the New Testament epistles, or the creeds of the church. Cragg accepts the distinction, made by New Testament criticism in the modern era, between historical facts about Jesus of Nazareth and beliefs about him developed by the church. For Cragg it is essential to present to Muslims what Jesus taught and did, carefully distinguishing the self-understanding of Christ from the beliefs in Christ held by the church.

In order to present the historical Jesus to Muslims it is also necessary for Christians to begin with what Muslims already know about him from the Qur'ān, for a Christology that does not take account of Islamic convictions about Christ will not be properly understood, let alone accepted, by Muslims. Cragg's way of using the Qur'ān is new in Christian apologetics for, unlike those before him, he seeks to get back behind developed Christology to the kind of person the historical Jesus claimed to be.

The Call of the Minaret

Cragg's earliest attempt at communicating a Christian view of Jesus to Muslims was made in his first book *The Call of the Minaret*, written in 1956 while he was teaching at Hartford Seminary in Connecticut, USA. He had served as a curate in the Church of England before moving to Beirut in 1939 to teach philosophy in the American University there. The book reflects his situation as an educator of Western postgraduate scholars of Islam and is addressed to Christians who seek to relate to Muslims in the Islamic world. In the light of his own exposure to the Islamic world he encourages Western Christians to identify as much as possible with Muslims in their thinking and communicating. In terms of Christology this means that Christian talk about Jesus must be done in terms that Muslims can understand, relating to Christ in the same way that the first disciples did. They came to convictions about him after a period of time rather than all at once, and Muslims may need to be allowed some considerable time to appreciate who Jesus claimed to be.

Cragg expounds the significance of Jesus from an evangelical Protestant perspective that emphasises the effect of his death for others. Cragg has more in common with Pfander than liberal gospel scholars who deny that Jesus intended to die for others. His failure to acknowledge such scholarship opens his writing to the same criticism that Pfander had faced a century previously, that the picture of Christ is not one that is truly representative of Christian opinion.

Cragg might have argued that many distinguished gospel scholars held that Jesus did intend to go to the cross on behalf of others, but he seems unwilling to get drawn into Christian scholarly debate. However, this lack of attention to internal discussion among Christians is a serious problem for a presentation of Jesus for Muslims.

In 1976 Cragg was invited by the World Council of Churches to represent them in a debate on mission at Chambèsy, Switzerland. Cragg had established himself as the leading Christian exponent of dialogue with Muslims, not only through the widely read *The Call of the Minaret*, but also in his 1959 work, *Sandals at the Mosque*. The very titles of these books suggested a peaceful, eirenic attitude on his part to Islamic convictions. Cragg was summoning fellow Christians to a serious listening exercise, and was the obvious choice for the leadership of the kind of high profile event that the WCC dialogue section had in mind. Ismā'īl al-Farūqī was also an obvious leader of the Muslim delegation at the talks. He had taught religious studies in several North American Universities, and had established a reputation as a Muslim student of Christianity. Cragg concentrates in this debate on the logic of incarnation, since the character of God is at stake when presenting a Christian view of Jesus and his own evaluation of the debate points out the strategic importance he placed on the doctrine of God in discussion with Muslims concerning Christ. He was unwilling to accept that the Qur'ān reveals an adequate way of finding forgiveness with God. Dialogue then, for Christians, is the opportunity to make clear the conviction that God was in Christ reconciling the world to himself. Other ways of reconciliation are not true ways, and it is the task of Christians to clarify this in dialogue with Muslims.

Jesus and the Muslim

Cragg wrote *Jesus and the Muslim* in 1985 to meet an unfulfilled need "to have the New Testament seriously read and studied in the Islamic world". He is more concerned to get to the heart of Jesus' ministry, than to engage in a defence of the historicity of the miracle stories of the gospels. Echoing the thinking of *The Call of the Minaret*, he sees the verse "the Son of Man must suffer" (Mark 8:31) as the secret to all that motivated Jesus, whose determination to face the hostility of religious vested interests is the outward expression of this inner commitment.

He attempts to build his Christology on the historical records contained in the synoptic gospels. This marks him out from ninth century apologists as a twentieth century European Christian who is unwilling to base Christology on church tradition. He never appeals to credal formulations in his dialogical work in the way that ninth century writers did. Cragg begins with Jesus the preacher of the kingdom, and the doer of compassionate deeds for those in need. He is representative of a movement away from doing Christology from 'above' to 'below', away from the incarnation of the eternal Son, to the human Jesus who is recognised as being in a unique relationship with God.

While aware of radical criticism of the gospels Cragg is not inclined to shift from his early conviction that, from the beginning of his ministry, Jesus set his face to Jerusalem to die for recalcitrant humanity. What the disciples came to see in him was not a product of their imagination but recognition of his divine character. It is this realisation that Muslims need to arrive at too, so Cragg applies his energy to bring about a Muslim awakening to the 'real' Jesus, obscured by the Qur'ān and centuries of tradition.

He shares with Pfander an evangelical theology of forgiveness only through the cross and appeals to the incarnation as an act of condescension on God's part. Jesus reveals a God who suffers human weakness. He embodies God's kingdom as a rule of love.

In the final analysis, the Christology in *Jesus and the Muslim* is not essentially different from that found in *The Call of the Minaret* 30 years earlier. However, in the context of Muslim response to this Christology, Cragg has neither made much room for scholarly issues concerning the facts of the life of Jesus, nor for the challenge laid down by al-Farūqī concerning the freedom of God to limit himself.

The Christologies of John Hick and Hans Küng in Dialogue with Muslims

Kenneth Cragg's engagement with Islam arose from early exposure to the Muslim world of the Middle East, enabling him to develop a thorough understanding of the Islamic challenge to Christology. However, among European theologians his experience is rare. John Hick and Hans Küng are more typical of the recent interaction of Western theology and Islam. Both men were established theological writers before attempting to communicate with Muslims, and their Christological views were already developed for a Western context. The fact that they turned their attention to a global context for theology demonstrates a shift in the self-understanding of some Western Christian leaders away from simply doing theology in the traditionally Christian world of Europe and North America, to thinking about the Christian faith in non-Christian contexts.

In Hick's case the presence of Muslims in the United Kingdom urged him to rethink a theology worked out in training for the Presbyterian ministry in England and subsequent lecturing in theological faculties of North American and British universities. For Küng, a career as a theological lecturer in the University of Tübingen in Germany intersected with Islam through visits to the Muslim world in which he attempted to build bridges between Christianity and Islam. Both men were also concerned to relate Christian thought to other major religious traditions and attempted to dialogue with Hindus and Buddhists as well as with Muslims. Neither is an expert in Islamic thought, having no first-hand knowledge of Arabic to read original Islamic texts, and the published dialogues they led were conducted in English with Muslim scholars familiar to Western university teaching. Hick and Küng are representative of a new reality in Christian thought, which is likely to be increasingly relevant in the twenty-first century, as Christian theologians will continue to feel the need to address an Islamic context when articulating Christology.

John Hick's Christology

John Hick (1922-2012) came relatively late to communicating a view of Jesus to Muslims. Having taught philosophy of religion in the USA since the 1950s, it was not until he occupied the H.G. Wood chair of Theology at Birmingham University in 1967 that he began to dialogue with Muslims. His new awareness of other faiths was to bring about a 'Copernican revolution' in his thinking about Christ, which was a shift from Christocentrism to Theocentrism. An exposition of this shift comes at the beginning of a series of papers given at a trialogue of Christians, Muslims and Jews in September 1981, convened and chaired by Hick himself.

According to his own testimony at the trialogue, Hick at one time held that the incarnation, trinity and atonement were divinely revealed truths, but that he gradually came to accept that these concepts were better understood as products of human thinking. The implications of gospel scholarship for Christian theology are obvious to Hick. Jesus must be seen as a man exceptionally conscious of God's presence, but not as God become human. Jesus was not unique in his capacity to relate truth about God. Hick came to see that other great religious figures, including Muhammad, were just as 'God conscious' as Jesus was. Therefore, he believed that it was no longer right for Christians to regard Islam as inferior but rather Christians should view Islam as complementary to Christianity. Love for the Muslim neighbour demanded no less.

It is hardly surprising that Hick should be criticised by more traditional Christians for his severe reductionism. In a response to such criticism in his 1995 *The Rainbow of Faiths*, Hick defends his scepticism about much of the material in the gospels. The book is written in the form of dialogues between Hick and a philosopher 'Phil' and a theologian 'Grace'.

Hick acknowledges that possible interpretations arise out of pre-suppositions, suggesting that if you want biblical confirmation for a conservative position, you can find it, and if you want biblical confirmation for a more liberal position you can find that as well. Hick's pre-supposition is that the divinity of Jesus proclaimed within the New Testament by John and Paul has to be set aside for pragmatic reasons. However, the very pragmatism at work in relation to those of other faiths fails to take account of the fact that the Christian tradition has been indelibly shaped by John and Paul.

Hick tries to persuade traditional Christians that the Apostolic and Patristic faith in Christ as human and divine is not founded on fact and therefore is not true. Yet Hick's dialogue with other Christians may be fruitless except in producing alienation and enmity, since these Christians hold that their faith in Christ is the logical outcome of tendencies in the life and teaching of the historical Jesus. This is the position of the Catholic theologian, Hans Küng, who comes somewhere between Cragg and Hick in his Christology in dialogue with Muslims.

In the desire to make himself a good neighbour, Hick has not really considered two consequences of his friendly overtures. In the case of Muslims, the fact that Hick is unwilling to endorse the conviction that everything the Qur'ān says is true puts him at odds with a fifth of the world's population. In what sense then does Hick love his Muslim neighbour, when he cannot affirm this essential item in Islam?

The second consequence concerns Hick's ability to represent the Christian third of the world's population. The condemnation of the vast majority of Christians to an inevitable conflict with Muslims because of their faith in the incarnation and atonement seems premature. Pluralist and traditionalist Christians are equally capable of being good neighbours to people of other faiths, because although they see Jesus differently, they are able to love Muslims despite such differences. Love for Muslims is not dependent on theology alone.

Hans Küng's Christology

Hans Küng (b. 1928) has been a professor of theology at the University of Tübingen in Germany since 1960. He was an active participant in the proceedings of Vatican II in the early 1960s, and has promoted the new understanding of the Catholic Church concerning people of other faiths that emerged from the Council. In 1985 he published *Christianity and World Religions* without having engaged in much encounter with Muslims, although the book opened the path to engagement with Muslims outside Germany.

Christianity and World Religions

In *Christianity and World Religions* Küng believes it is vital to begin with the portrait of Jesus given in the Qur'ān in conversation with Muslims. For the Qur'ān Jesus is a prophet but nothing more. And just as in the New Testament John the Baptist is Jesus' precursor, so in the Qur'ān Jesus is the precursor for Muḫammad. This does not mean that Küng is content to stay with the Jesus of the Qur'ān, since he believes it is essential to challenge Muslims to accept the historical Jesus of the gospels.

In 1984 Küng was asked to engage in dialogue at Harvard University with a leading Muslim scholar, Seyyed Hossein Nasr of George Washington University. Nasr's response to Küng's was that for Muslims, "the Qur'ān, the whole Qur'ān and not only parts of it, is the word of God." At the end of Nasr's response Küng had the opportunity to reply to Nasr's criticisms. "Let us say that the Gospels are wrong, and that the whole New Testament is wrong, that Jesus has not really been crucified. To say this from a source which comes from the seventh century is for an historically thinking man, I think, personally impossible."

Nasr seems to be comfortable with the notion that Islam is only one version of truth, but he is not prepared to allow the validity of alternative sources of truth that would contradict revelation as Islam understands it. Küng believes that Christology can commence from the Qur'ān before ending up in the New Testament. As long as

Christians set aside the convictions of the creeds, there can be a genuine conversation with Muslims about Jesus.

In the light of his view that Islam provides salvation without a specifically Christian understanding of Jesus, do Muslims really need Jesus the way Christians need him? Küng made himself famous in Roman Catholic circles for his 1964 address in Bombay in which he expounded the new view of Vatican II that, "God's saving will also embraces those who acknowledge the Creator and among them especially the Muslims, who profess the faith of Abraham and together with us adore the one God, the Merciful One, who will judge men on the Last Day." Küng put forward the idea that Christianity is the 'extraordinary' way of salvation and the other religions are 'ordinary' ways. In 1994 he re-affirmed his belief in these two ways of salvation.

> *For me as a Christian – to speak quite plainly here – Jesus Christ is and remains the way, the truth and the life (that is as it were my internal perspective), but (and this is at the same time my external perspective) I cannot avoid noting that 'the way, the truth, and the life' is for believing Jews the Torah, for Muslims the Qur'ān and for other religions someone or something else.*

But then the question arises, why worry about communicating a Christian view of Jesus to Muslims if there is no need for them to depart from a Qur'ānic basis of faith? Perhaps Küng should be content to explain a Christian view in dialogue without challenging the Islamic view of the crucifixion as he has done. Why should the Qur'ān stand accused of flying in the face of history? If the Qur'ān is an adequate vehicle for salvation then history hardly counts, and if Muslims can find God through Islam then they do not need to be told that their means of salvation is somehow less than adequate. Küng might reply that the Qur'ānic portrait of Jesus is not adequate but that God is able to reveal truth, redeem sinners, and liberate oppressed humans through the Qur'ān, despite the denial of the crucifixion. Perhaps he would say that the New Testament is a more complete account of revelation, redemption and liberation, and that the point of communicating the Christ of the Bible is to offer that fuller version of salvation to Muslims.

Küng, Hick and Cragg on Christology in Dialogue with Muslims

These three theologians share the common late twentieth century theological conviction that the Christological formulations of Nicaea and Chalcedon are no longer useful for Christology, since they emphasise being rather than doing, static nature rather than active commitment. Cragg can speak for all three when he says,

> *We return from Chalcedon to Gethsemane and to a Christology of action as sufficing for a Christology of nature ... It is interesting to note that the Creeds and Chalcedonian Christology had ... no required theology of atonement. Content with the fact of the Cross they left the preaching of it to the Holy Spirit in the mind of the Church. It might have been well to have done the same with the incarnation had not Gnosticism and other perils needed refutation for there to be any authentic redemption at all.*

Cragg's Christology is about the self-giving of Jesus to reconcile humanity to God. This picture is dependent on the truth that Jesus alone among human beings is God in human flesh. Only the self-giving of God expressed in Christ redeems others from alienation to God. However, this incarnational Christology depends on the very ontological Nicene thought patterns that Cragg wishes to move away from, which only shows the difficulty of separating ontological and functional categories in Christology.

Küng's Christology focuses on the life of Jesus rather than his atoning death. Indeed, Küng hardly mentions the atonement at all in dialogue with Muslims, preferring to emphasise that Jesus of Nazareth represented God in his teaching and actions. This is seen especially in his authority to forgive sin directly and in his promulgation of an ethic of self-denial. He believes that Muslims can benefit from adopting this Jesus, who transcends the one they already know from the Qur'ān. The knowledge of God's forgiveness and the life of self-denial need to become part of Islamic life. The cross of Christ can then become a symbol of forgiveness and self-giving rather than a symbol of God-forsakenness and human weakness.

Hick's Christology differs radically from those of Cragg and Küng. The real Jesus did not represent God in a unique way. He was a Jew who advocated love for God and neighbour in the spirit of the best of Jewish tradition. Muslims are just as capable of loving God and neighbour as Christians, since the Qur'ān emphasises these virtues. Dialogue ought to enable Christians and Muslims to work together to promote a common cause. Therefore it should be possible for Christians to overlook the denial of the crucifixion of Jesus in the Qur'ān, seeing that this historical detail is not essential to bringing about love for God and neighbour. Cragg's incarnational Christology gets in the way of a meeting of minds, and Küng's Jesus who uniquely represents God is not much better because he excludes any other humans from representing God in the same way. Hick is much closer to an Islamic way of seeing Jesus than Küng or Cragg, but he speaks for a much smaller number of Christians than they do. Nevertheless, the appropriation of New Testament scholarly debate on the historical Jesus by all three shows the importance of the 'real' Jesus to twentieth century theology. In the context of dialogue with Muslims, all three have drawn attention to material in the Qur'ān that supports the 'real' Jesus of the gospels.

In the final analysis, Cragg, Küng and Hick have not developed Christology on the basis of the Qur'ān, but rather have attempted to present a view of Christ already formed before interaction with the new context of Islamic ideas. However, their encounter with the Christ of Muslim faith has led them to draw various connections between Islamic perceptions and Christian ones. Cragg is more skilled at this task than Küng or Hick, and offers fresh ways for Muslims to see Christ by attempting to combine Islamic thought with mainstream Christian doctrine. This attempt on the part of Christians to suggest new insights to Muslims about their own traditions is taken probably as far as it may go by a dramatic version of the life of Christ based on the four gospels that was produced in 1987 for Muslim Arabs.

The Portrait of Christ in *Sīra al-Masīh̲*

A new Arabic harmonisation of the four gospels appeared in 1987, which presented the life of Christ using Islamic terminology and Qur'ānic style. The story of Jesus is divided into thirty chapters each headed by "in the name of God the merciful and compassionate one", combining material from all four gospels into one biographical account. It is written in rhyme with verse endings borrowed from the Qur'ān, and throughout the story, key words and phrases from the Qur'ān appear that are not found in standard translations of the gospels. This work takes the Qur'an more actively into the telling of the life of Christ than any of the apologetic writing surveyed so far, though the eighth century *Anonymous Apology* and the presentation of Christ by Kenneth Cragg offer the closest parallels in terms of using Islamic thought forms. In other words, this life of Christ is the most notable Christian attempt in the history of Christian-Muslim relations to view Christ from both Muslim and Christian perspectives.

The production of the work began in 1977 with the collaboration of several Christians from Orthodox, Catholic and Protestant backgrounds, under the leadership of a Christian Palestinian poet and an American Protestant missionary. Their working method was based on the belief that the Qur'ān could furnish words and ideas for a Christian life of Christ as a significant, albeit incomplete, witness to God's Messiah.

This admission represents a fundamental paradigm shift for both the American Evangelical David Owen and for the Middle Eastern Christians involved in the writing of *The Life of Christ*. Although David Owen believed that it faithfully translated the original Greek of the gospels into Arabic, perhaps it should be seen as an exercise in indigenous theology for Arabs from a Muslim background, since Qur'ānic language is used in the translation in an unprecedented way. For example, the use of the Qur'ānic name *`Īsā* for Jesus in *The Life of Christ* is a startling innovation for Christian Arabic writing, where the ancient Syriac *Yasu`a* is normally found (although not totally unprecedented in Christian writing in Arabic) and sends a signal to the Muslim reader that *`Īsā* of the Qur'ān is the subject of the story.

The *`Īsā* of *Sīra* is clearly recognisable to a Christian familiar with the New Testament. The birth of *`Īsā* is basically the account in Matthew and Luke, with details derived from *Sūra* 19 of the Qur'ān. The teaching of *`Īsā* is co-extensive with all four gospels, with little from the fourth gospel omitted. His healing work and his raising the dead are fully documented. The Qur'ān has, of course, little to add to his teaching, but it is significant that the miracle of the making of birds from clay is not found in *Sīra*. To the Muslim reader this signals that *Sīra* is unwilling to acknowledge the veracity of a story about *`Īsā* found in the Qur'ān.

What is significant about *Sīra*'s Christology is the way the four gospels are adapted for a Muslim readership. While the Qur'ān is not the foundation of the portrait, it does have an influence on the way

`*Īsā* is actually presented. Attention paid to what the Qur'ān denies about `*Īsā* makes *Sīra* the most penetrating attempt so far by Christians to retell the story of Jesus in a way that might commend itself to Muslims. This is most obvious in the rewriting of the Father-Son language. The great tradition of Christian apologetics to Muslims has attempted to explain the Father-Son language. *Sīra* goes beyond this impasse by virtually removing the metaphor. Where Father-Son language is used, the context shows that the relationship is a spiritual one. While an argument may be made for more Father-Son language to be retained, there can be no reasonable doubt that *Sīra* has succeeded in removing a psychological obstacle in the mind of the Muslim reader. If apologists have always insisted that the relationship between Father and Son is only spiritual and never physical, then *Sīra* has removed the need to make the argument. This is a considerable gain.

Another gain for *Sīra* is the careful handling of the Johannine language identifying Jesus as God. The simple removal of "the Word was God" from the story enables Jesus' claim to be "one with the Father" to become a unity of thought or will. This has far reaching consequences for the Muslim reader. Since Jesus is not actually identified with God in *Sīra*, a Muslim reader is enabled to experience him in a familiar monotheistic framework. With the removal of explicit references to Jesus' identity of being with God, it becomes possible for a Muslim to be in the same position as a Jew in Jesus' own time. The question for both Jew and Muslim is, "How does this Jesus relate to the one true God?" *Sīra* makes the point particularly strongly that `*Īsā* volunteers to die according to the will of God. His death is no accident but is right at the centre of what he is trying to achieve in his life of service.

In summary, this retelling of the story of Christ is a fresh and original attempt to attract Muslim readers to an essentially Christian narrative. By taking seriously the challenge concerning the sonship of Christ emanating from the Qur'ān, *Sīra* may enable Muslims to see the Christian claims about Christ from a new angle. This is an important advance in Christian-Muslim dialogue on Christ and may be the opening for other Christian initiatives in the future. Conversely, the Qur'ānic denial of the crucifixion is dealt with in *Sīra* not by displacement but by counterclaim. Whereas Christ hardly calls himself God's son, he repeats the prediction of his impending crucifixion more frequently in *Sīra* than in the gospels. Perhaps this risk is too great, since the Muslim reader is far more likely to be offended by the repetition than he would by a more veiled account of the death of Christ.

The Christologies of Kenneth Cragg, John Hick, Hans Küng and Sīra al-Masīḫ, and Muslim Response

The two questions asked of the ninth century apologists in chapter six may be profitably posed to their twentieth century equivalents. Firstly, what developments in Christology can be observed as a result of engagement with the Islamic context? Secondly, what impact did these presentations of Christology have on Muslims? The answer to the first question in the ninth century apologetics was little development in content but a considerable effort to defend established Christology in terms that Muslims might find acceptable. The answer now is similar. Cragg, Hick and Küng do not alter their Christologies to any extent in the Islamic context, but they do attempt to defend their established views in ways that might be understood by Muslims. *Sīra al-Masīḫ*, however, is more an original appoach to Christology from within an Islamic context, rather than an already established view applied to it. The answer to the second question can be found in the dialogue partners of the three modern apologists. Only Hick's Christology is enthusiastically received for his acceptance of Islamic premises for the interpretation of Christ's significance.

The Christology of Kenneth Cragg

Cragg presents to Muslims the incarnation and atonement as essentially true for them as much as for Christians. From *The Call of the Minaret* to *Jesus and the Muslim* he believes that Muslims need to believe in the revelation of God in Christ rather than merely the speech of God in Christ's mouth. In his dialogue with al-Farūqī, Cragg puts forward the argument about personal revelation in incarnation as essential for Muslims to accept. The central point of *Jesus and the Muslim* is 'truth through personality' though he acknowledges that the notion is difficult for Muslims to accept.

He presses Muslims to accept that personal revelation is the only means of divine identification with sinful humanity. But this focus on the atonement comes up against the fact that the death of Christ is denied by the Qur'ān. Christians should proclaim that the cross is not the failure of God's prophet, but the door to victory over all that might defeat God's rule in the world he made. At the heart of personal revelation is the forgiveness of sin. If according to Islam God forgives without the cost of coming into relationship with sinful humans, then that forgiveness is not nearly so profound as that which is offered through the death of the Incarnate Christ.

Future dialogue would be better served by avoiding such direct assault on Islamic thought, perhaps by arguing that God was under no necessity to forgive through the cross, but that he chose to show his compassion to humanity through the death of Christ. Cragg does speak for the vast majority of Christians who uphold the Apostolic convictions of the incarnation and atonement and they will continue to find inspiration from his determined efforts to persuade Muslims that God was in Christ reconciling humans to himself.

The Christology of John Hick

Hick's Christology is much more likely to be received warmly by Muslims than Cragg's since Jesus is aligned with other prophets in status, but at the same time is unlikely to be accepted by most Christians who view Christ as much more than a prophet. In the final analysis, by confining Christ to being an exemplar for the spiritual experience of others, Hick parts company with mainstream Christians who continue to uphold the incarnation and atonement as true, and therefore he does not represent majority Christian opinion in dialogue with Muslims. Hick's pioneering Christology leaves him exposed on the fringes of Christianity with the result that he can only speak for a small number of like-minded theologians. Thus while providing an attractive portrait of Christ from a Muslim point of view, Hick may mislead Muslims into thinking that he is in the vanguard of a new approach to Christology that will become increasingly accepted by other Christians when this is unlikely to be the case.

The Christology of Hans Küng

Küng comes somewhere between Cragg and Hick in his estimation of Christ. He believes that the incarnation was an Apostolic overlay on the much more modest claims of Jesus of Nazareth, who was proclaimed Son of God only after his death and resurrection. Certainly, Küng's desire to eliminate ontology from Christology is likely to find a warm response from Muslims, but his denial of the Apostolic faith in the essentially divine character of Christ distances him from most Christians.

Like Cragg he thinks history must win the argument over theology, though unlike Cragg he does not insist that God's forgiveness comes through the historical event of the death of Christ. Forgiveness may be granted by God to Muslims without the mediation of Christ's death as a sacrifice for sin, so the value of Christ's death lies rather in the expession of God's love in the self-giving of Jesus, and the assurance that God is involved in human suffering to bring new meaning and hope.

Küng then rejects Cragg's insistence on the incarnation and atonement as essential to Christology and to ongoing relations with Muslims. On the other hand, he disagrees with Hick's reading of Jesus' attitude to Jewish law, and to his setting aside of the death of Jesus. Both of these details from the gospels must be upheld by Christians as historical facts and cannot merely be regarded as interpretations of Jesus' life that are negotiable because Muslims do not approve. On the contrary, one of the tasks of genuine dialogue between Christians and Muslims is to get consensus on the facts of history, and Muslims have to be persuaded that this is essential to good relations between the two faith communities.

Like Hick, Küng has been interested in relationships between Christians and people of many different faiths rather than merely Christian relations with Muslims, so his Christology reflects this wider audience. Küng's Christology departs from mainstream Catholic doctrine which continues to insist on the incarnation and atonement as essential to faith in Christ, and therefore his ability to represent his own church community in dialogue with Muslims is put in question.

The Christology of Sīra al-Masīh

The Christ of *Sīra al-Masīh* is similar to the Christ of the gospels in many respects. He performs the same miracles, tells the same stories, makes similar authoritative pronouncements in God's name, and sets himself on a collision course with Jewish leaders that leads to his arrest and crucifixion. However, he rarely calls God his Father and never refers to himself as Son of man. His followers never call him Son of God as they often do in the gospels. *Sīra*'s Christ has no identity of being with God, although he does appear to have an eternal relationship with him. Without doubt *Sīra* has presented a form of incarnation tailored to Muslim sensibilities over ideas of sonship. This imaginative reshaping of the gospel story avoids the need to advance an apologetic for traditional gospel language as Cragg and Küng have done.

Sīra has gone beyond anything seen in the history of Christian-Muslim dialogue. Cragg and Küng stand outside the Islamic world in their thinking, and do not hesitate to judge the Qur'ān as containing an erroneous portrait of Christ. *Sīra* is composed from within the Islamic world by Christians fully aware of the reality of life as a minority in an Islamic milieu. Only *Sīra*, among modern presentations of Christ for Muslims, has accepted the full responsibility of speaking about Christ in terms that Muslims may receive without instantly rejecting as unsound. Muslims may well find this portrait congenial to their perceptions of Christ in such a way that they are enabled to see the fuller life of Christ found in the gospels as completing the summary details in the Qur'ān.

The very telling of the story makes use of Islamic language to suggest to Muslim readers another interpretation of the denial of Christ's death. Still, the denial of the crucifixion may not so easily be undone by *Sīra*'s transformation of negation to affirmation and the basic contradiction between gospel testimony and Qur'ānic counter-claim remains a continuing problem for Christian-Muslim dialogue.

Nevertheless, *Sīra* has not replaced standard translations of the gospels in Arabic, and therefore has a limited role among Arabic speaking Christians. Whether such a contextual version of the gospels can become more widely accepted by Christians remains to be seen. In other words, Arab Muslims, who may be drawn to the Christ presented in *Sīra*, are still faced with the traditional portrait prized by Arab Christians as a whole with all the problems inherent in the established versions of the gospels that *Sīra* has attempted to overcome. Once again, creative theology in dialogue comes up against traditional modes of expressing faith held by the majority to be essential.

Muslim Responses to Christian Views of Christ in the Twentieth Century

The Muslim dialogue partners of Cragg and Küng, al-Farūqī and Nasr, both base their understanding of Christ on the Qur'ānic portrait. Cragg's challenge to al-Farūqī to make room for the possibility of incarnation as part of God's freedom of action is met by the warning that God has revealed in the Qur'ān that certain divine actions are inconceivable as contradictory to the character of God. Christ must be seen as human but not divine.

Nasr objects to Küng's criticisms of the Qur'ān by asserting that for all Muslims without exception the whole of the Qur'ān is the word of God and not just certain parts of it. If Christians want to dialogue with Muslims then they will have to adhere to this principle, otherwise no serious conversation can take place.

The approach of Cragg and Küng to the Qur'ān is not likely to be the best way forward for twenty-first century dialogue between Christians and Muslims, because any direct challenge to the authority of the Qur'ān simply frustrates genuine dialogue. A more fruitful approach to dialogue could arise if Christians were to develop concepts and arguments for their Christology from the teaching of the Qur'ān in the way that *Sīra* has done.

Conclusion

Developments in Christology are seen in the way Islamic concerns are addressed by the Christian apologists. Cragg has a more thorough understanding of Muslim thought than Küng or Hick and thinks the main issue for dialogue is an inadequate Muslim view of the transendence of God. If Muslims could accept that transendence includes immanence then the incarnation would become intelligible for them. For Cragg, the development is not so much in Christology as in the doctrine of God. Küng and Hick leave behind an incarnational Christology as no longer acceptable for modern Christians who want to dialogue with people of other faiths. Küng thinks that the early Apostolic belief that Jesus was adopted by God can be retained but that the later ideas of eternal sonship and ontological equality between Christ and God must be discarded. Christ reveals the authority of God in his teaching, the power of God in his healings, and the love of God in his death. He believes that this more semitic Christology will appeal to Muslims. Hick thinks that this portrait is still too far removed from the real Jesus who was only a human channel for God's authority, power and love. He claimed no unique divine qualities for himself. If Christians could jettison the whole Apostolic superstructure placed on Jesus then relations with people of other faiths would dramatically improve, and Christians would be able to accept other religious leaders, such as Muhammad, on equal terms with Christ. Küng and Hick do not address Islamic thought in isolation from other religious worldviews, though they believe that their Christologies foster dialogue with Muslims. *Sīra* presents Christ as an obedient servant of God who is able to teach with divine authority, perform mighty divine deeds, and die as a means of bringing God's forgiveness to wayward humans. There are hints of him having an eternal origin and equality of status with God, but these are not emphasised to allow Muslims to appreciate this Christian life of Christ without rejecting it outright. Here Muslim perceptions meet gospel scholarship to produce a contextualised life of Christ that makes a unique contribution to Christian/Muslim dialogue.

The response by the Muslim dialogue partners shows that any insistence on aspects of Christology that contradict the Qur'ānic account of Christ fails to convince. Cragg's reinterpretation of transcendence is unacceptable to al-Farūqī because the Qur'ān does not support it. God cannot become human on any sane reading of the Qur'ān, and Christians ought not to give misleading Qur'ānic interpretations in dialogue with Muslims. Küng's accusation that the Qur'ān is wrong about the cross offends Nasr who points out that dialogue should be conducted on non-polemical principles. Hick's eirenic approach to Islamic ideas hides a more aggressive tone when Siddiqi challenges him to admit the truth of divine revelation. Hick's failure to acknowledge revelation on Islamic terms counts against his seemingly more Islamic account of Christ. *Sīra*'s attempt to turn the Qur'ānic denial of the crucifixion into a prediction of the cross would probably be regarded by Muslims as completely illegitimate.

On the other hand, Muslims do appreciate the Christian effort to reinterpret Christ in human terms. Nasr hails Küng and Siddiqi applauds Hick for taking Islamic convictions seriously in their presentations of Christ. Certainly their very human Jesus is more acceptable to Muslims as a starting point for dialogue than Cragg's Incarnate Christ, whose humanity is rather muted in the process of carrying out of his divine mission to redeem humanity. *Sīra*'s hidden Incarnate Christ could therefore be helpful in dialogue with Muslims, since Christ speaks and acts as one called by God to serve his people. While it is true that *Sīra*'s Christ sometimes suggests that he acts on the basis of a divine status, for the most part he is recognisably human to a Muslim reader. There is much then to be gained in dialogue on Christology by presenting the life of Christ in such a way that Muslims can meet the Christ of history before they are asked to consider the faith of the Church in him.

Conclusion
Prospects for Dialogue on Christology

Future dialogue about Christ between Christians and Muslims will depend on the way the Qur'ānic denials of sonship and the crucifixion and the developed Islamic conviction that the incarnation is impossible are dealt with. Perhaps the first of these issues is simpler to handle, but the historicity of the cross and the transcendence of God disallowing incarnation are much more demanding. As a result of these seemingly unbridgable differences between Muslims and Christians, some voices are calling for dialogue to avoid Christology and to concentrate on the ethical teaching of Jesus instead. However, the authority of Jesus' teaching depends on the assessment made of his status, and that takes dialogue back to the question of the revelation of God in Jesus, unless appeal is made solely to human reason.

The Ethics of Jesus

Since belief in the status of Christ causes dispute between Christians and Muslims it might seem simpler to avoid dialogue on his status and discuss his teaching instead. The leading American Catholic theologian on inter-faith dialogue, Paul Knitter, has proposed that debate about doctrine should give way to dialogue on behaviour. According to Knitter, belief in Christ is "primarily a matter of acting with and like Christ." Christians should live out the kingdom of God that Jesus proclaimed as a "spirit-filled mystic and a social prophet." Knitter has had more experience in dialogue with Hindus and Buddhists, but his call is echoed by Pierre Claverie, Catholic Bishop of Oran in Algeria. In a letter entitled 'Believing in Dialogue' he indicates five fruitful issues for Christian-Muslim dialogue: submission to God, secularism, democracy, the role of women, and the status of non-Muslims. All five subjects relate to personal and social ethics, since submission to God, in Claverie's mind, has to do with behaviour rather than belief. Agreement on the ethics of Jesus may remain a challenge for Christians if the debate between Hick and Küng about Jesus' attitude to the Jewish law continues to divide interpreters of the gospels. Division among Muslims about the contemporary relevance of Qur'ānic law may well be a feature of twenty-first century Islam. If Claverie's topics are discussed, Muslims will probably be as divided over each of them as Christians over the teaching of Jesus. Therefore, dialogue on the teaching of Jesus will be no more straightforward than dialogue on his status. The authority of his teaching will have to be faced when a clash between his teaching and Islamic tradition emerges. Whether Muslims will be prepared to grant him the authority to challenge Islamic norms is a difficult question to answer. It is because Christians believe in the divine status of Christ that they grant him the authority to instruct them – so in the end, dialogue on the teaching of Christ cannot avoid dialogue on Christology.

Final Words

There were different strategies in dialogue on Christology in the ninth and twentieth centuries. Some drew heavily on Christian tradition and attempted to commend received views of Christ in terms Muslims might understand if not accept. In the modern period, others developed fresh ways of perceiving Christ and offered their new insights to Muslims. Both ninth and twentieth century apologists took Islamic concerns seriously enough to challenge Muslims to rethink their perception of Christ, but there were no major breakthroughs over the denial of the cross or the divinity of Christ. In terms of future dialogue on Christ it may be possible to bypass these difficulties by discussing the ethics of Jesus. However, if Muslims question his authority to teach there will be a continuing need for creative Christology in dialogue with Muslims.

Short Bibliography

Mark Beaumont, *Jesus in Muslim-Christian Conversation* (Cascade Books: Eugene, OR, 2018)

Kenneth Cragg, *Jesus and the Muslim* (Oxford: Oneworld, 1999).

John Hick, *The Rainbow of Faiths* (London: SCM, 1995)

Tarif Khalidi, *The Muslim Jesus* (Cambridge: Harvard University Press, 2001)

Hans Kung, *Islam* (Oxford: Oneworld, 2007)

Mona Siddiqui, *Christians, Muslims, & Jesus* (New Haven and London: Yale University Press, 2013)

David E. Singh (ed), *Jesus and the Cross: Reflections of Christians from Islamic Contexts* (Oxford: Regnum, 2008)

David E. Singh (ed), *Jesus and the Incarnation: Reflections of Christians from Islamic Contexts* (Oxford: Regnum, 2011)

David E. Singh (ed), *Jesus and the Resurrection:Reflections of Christians from Islamic Contexts* (Oxford: Regnum, 2014)

A.H. Mathias Zahniser, *The Mission & Death of Jesus in Islam and Christianity* (New York: Orbis, 2008)

Regnum Mini-Books

Corruption and the Church | Martin Allaby

How do Christians in the global south see the relationship between the church and corruption? This book summarises the views of 101 leaders of churches, Christian faith-based organisations and anti-corruption organisations, as told during in-depth interviews with the author. Capturing voices from across three continents, this summary and analysis of their views makes for some uncomfortable reading, but suggests some constructive ways forward.

Deliver Us from Evil | Roberto Laver

Christians have been largely silent on the issue of corruption. Roberto Laver has been one of the few voices of the Christian community calling for the church to stand up and address this issue. Laver's scholarship undergirded by his faith and concern for the poor and marginalized, gives Christians a compelling wake-up call to confront this scourge. In so doing, he takes a big step toward filling a conspicuous gap in the literature of mission study and practice.

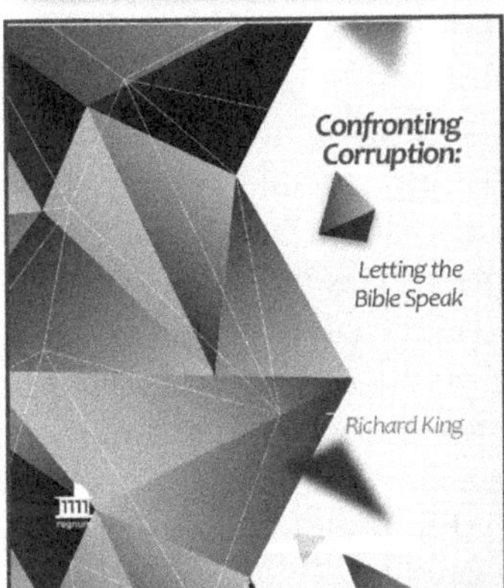

Confronting Corruption | Richard King

Corruption blights the lives of countless people around our world. The purpose of this book is to transform attitudes and behaviours of Christians who live in societies where corrupt behaviour is a fact of life and to do this by letting the Bible, as God's word, speak. The book is intended to be used for weekly reading by pastors at church services to remind congregations that corruption has no place in Christian life, as a resource for Bible colleges in training pastors/church workers and for small group Bible study.

Regnum Mini-Books

Unity & Reconciliation in Rwanda | S Cyuma

In the last ten years of the 20th century, the world was twice confronted with unbelievable news from Africa. Can we compare the situation in South Africa with that in Rwanda? Can Rwandan leaders draw lessons from the peace process in South Africa? These are some of the questions that this publication addresses.

Bridging the Cultural Gap | Ole Kirchheiner

This is an abridged version of Ole Kirchheiner's Regnum book, Culture and Christianity Negotiated in Hindu Society. Through an examination of the Nepali church the study pays special attention to the way ordinary Christians have been able to settle social and religious issues to live and work together with the traditional religious people of Nepal, and maintain a good family life.

Seeking Reconciliation | Peter Rowan

With a history of racial violence and in recent years, low-level ethnic tensions, the themes of peaceful coexistence and social harmony are recurring ones in the discourse of Malaysian society. In such a context, this book looks at the role of the church as a reconciling agent, arguing that a reconciling presence within a divided society necessitates an ethos of peacemaking. Such an ethos is created and sustained when Christians understand that their identity has been transformed in Jesus Christ.